CHRISTMAS

A Crowell Holiday Book

CHRISTMAS

Written and illustrated by
Barbara Cooney

THOMAS Y. CROWELL COMPANY, NEW YORK

CROWELL HOLIDAY BOOKS

Edited by Susan Bartlett Weber

Christmas! Everywhere people are getting ready for Christmas.

Behind closed doors children are planning surprises.

Delicious things are cooking in the kitchen.

Houses and churches are trimmed with green boughs.

Candles are lit.

Eyes shine.

People sing.

The days are cold. The nights are long. But the air is full of magic and bright with love.

Around the world Christian children are waiting impatiently to celebrate the birthday of a little Jewish boy. He was born long ago, in a faraway village, in a stable.

His name was Jesus of Nazareth.

When Jesus grew up, he became a great and wise teacher. He taught men to love God and to love each other. His teachings became the worldwide religion called Christianity.

It is Jesus' birthday that we call Christmas.

Christmas, the twenty-fifth of December, is a day of rejoicing.

Jesus was born nearly two thousand years ago in the country of Palestine. The story of his birth is written in the New Testament of the Bible. It is called the story of the Nativity.

Palestine, the home of the Jewish people, was then part of the huge Roman Empire. It was ruled by the Roman Emperor.

Not long before Jesus was born, the Emperor decided to count the people in his Empire. He ordered each house-holder to return to his home town to be counted.

In the village of Nazareth lived a humble carpenter named Joseph and his young wife Mary. Even though Mary

was soon to have a baby, she went with Joseph to the town where he had been born. Joseph belonged to the house of David. So they went to the city of David, which was Bethlehem.

Bethlehem was far to the south. It was a long, weary journey over desert and mountain.

When they reached Bethlehem, the streets were crowded with people who had come to be counted. The inn was full. The only place for Mary to rest was a stable.

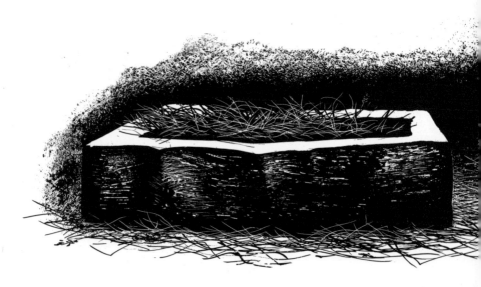

And so it happened, while they were in Bethlehem, that Mary's baby was born. For want of a cradle, she laid her son, wrapped in swaddling clothes, in the cattle's manger.

That same night there were shepherds watching their sheep in the country outside of Bethlehem. Suddenly the fields were lit with a bright and dazzling light. The shepherds became frightened. But an angel appeared and said to them:

"Fear not: for, behold, I bring you good tidings of great joy, which shall be to all people. For unto you is born this day, in the city of David, a Saviour, which is Christ the Lord. And this shall be a sign unto you: Ye shall find the babe wrapped in swaddling clothes, lying in a manger."

Then there was a rushing of wings and the sound of angel voices singing, "Glory to God in the highest, and on earth peace, good will toward men."

After the angels had disappeared, the shepherds hurried to Bethlehem. There, in the stable, they found the baby Jesus.

A great star hung in the sky that night. Far off in the east there were wise men who saw it. They thought it a sign that the Messiah, a new leader, had been born. And so, bearing gifts, they followed the star.

When they reached Jerusalem, the capital of Palestine, they asked, "Where is he that is born King of the Jews? For we have seen his star in the East, and are come to worship him."

When Herod, king of the Jews, heard of this, he was afraid that this new king might take his place. Gathering his priests about him, he asked where the child was born. And the priests answered, "In Bethlehem."

Next Herod sent for the wise men. "Go and search diligently for the young child," he said falsely, "and when you have found him, bring me word, that I may come and worship him also."

The wise men followed the star until it came to rest over the stable in Bethlehem. At the sight of the holy family, they rejoiced. They knelt before Jesus. In front of him they placed their gifts of gold and frankincense and myrrh.

But they did not return to Herod to tell him they had found the child. In a dream they were warned against him. Changing their plans, they went home by another way.

Herod, when he found he had been

tricked, was in a towering rage. He sent forth his men to slay all the baby boys in Bethlehem.

But Joseph, too, had a dream. An angel appeared and said, "Arise, and take the young child and his mother, and flee to Egypt; for Herod will seek the young child to destroy him."

So, in the dark of night, Joseph fled with Mary and Jesus to Egypt, where they were safe.

Today, in December, Christian families all around the world rejoice because Jesus was born. On December twenty-fifth they celebrate Jesus' birthday. But the celebrations begin before Christmas Day and last until Twelfth Night. On Twelfth Night, twelve days after Christmas, the holiday season ends.

To celebrate in December is an old, old custom. Long before the birth of Jesus there were midwinter festivals. When the long December nights began to grow shorter and the days started to grow longer, people celebrated the rebirth of the sun. These people, called pagans, worshipped the sun.

The peasants in northern Europe had a feast called Yule. A huge Yule log was brought in from the woods. As a symbol of the sun, it was blessed and burned with much ceremony.

During the Yule season the gray-bearded Norse god Odin was supposed to wander among his people. He came to reward and punish as he saw fit. He wore a blue cloak and a wide-brimmed hat pulled down over his one eye.

The ancient Romans had a December festival, too, the Saturnalia. It was named after Saturn, the Roman god of agriculture. It celebrated the return of the sun, as well as the rich harvest. A mock king, called Saturn like the god, was chosen to rule over the merry-makers during the festival.

The Saturnalia was a holiday for everyone. Schools were closed. Shops were shut. Houses and temples were decorated with green boughs and holly branches.

People dressed up in costumes and danced and feasted. They gave each other gifts of wax fruit, candles, and dolls.

Everyone enjoyed these December celebrations, including the first Christians. But the Christian Church did not approve of pagan customs that belonged to a time before the coming of Jesus. The Christians, however, did not want to give them up.

Finally, five hundred years after Jesus was born, the Church decided to celebrate Jesus' birthday in December. In this way, many of the merry pagan customs became part of the Christmas festival.

Over the years King Saturn of the Saturnalia became the Lord of Misrule. During the Middle Ages, the Lord of Misrule reigned during the Christmas season. In the castles and palaces there was gaiety and feasting while he was lord.

Odin's place was filled by St. Nicholas, another mysterious old man who came to reward good children. The first St. Nicholas was a kind and generous bishop who lived in the fourth century. Later this bishop became the patron saint of children.

St. Nicholas, riding a white pony, still visits children in Holland, Belgium, Switzerland, and parts of Austria and Germany.

Today, in the United States, we have Santa Claus. He is a white-bearded, round, and jolly little man who lives at the North Pole. There he and his helpers work all year, making toys.

On Christmas Eve, when all are asleep, Santa Claus sets out with his bulging

sack of toys. He flies over the rooftops in a sleigh drawn by eight reindeer. With a clattering of hooves, the reindeer halt on the housetops. Santa Claus alights. Then down the chimney he comes to fill the stockings of the children with toys and sweets.

Since pagan times the mid-December festival has been a festival of fire and light.

At Christmastime the Yule log is still burned in northern Europe.

Torches and bonfires are lit in many countries.

Fireworks are set off in Italy, France, and Spain.

Candlelight services are held in many Christian churches on Christmas Eve. Candles shine in the windows and on the altars.

In Sweden the first day of the Christmas season is called St. Lucia's Day. Before dawn a little girl goes from house to house, delivering coffee and cakes. She wears a white dress with a red sash. On her head rests a crown of lighted candles.

Lights shine on Christmas trees. Candles glow in windows. Fire and light, once symbols of the sun-god, now serve to brighten the way of the Christ Child.

We, too, use greens as did the ancient
Romans. We decorate our houses and

places of worship with evergreens and holly. We put wreaths on our doors. We hang mistletoe overhead.

As during the Saturnalia, friends are remembered and grudges forgotten. We send cards to our friends and wish them a merry Christmas.

For the people we love best, we buy or make presents. We tie them up in gay papers with shiny ribbons. Then, on Christmas Day, or on Christmas Eve, the packages are opened beside the Christmas tree.

We also feast and make merry. From kitchens come the good odors of Christmas cakes and cookies, of pies and puddings.

King Saturn feasted on boar's head. The Lord of Misrule smacked his lips over roasted peacock. But nothing is any finer than the plump, golden-brown turkey or goose we eat today.

At this happy time of year we sing songs of rejoicing, called carols, in churches and homes and in the streets.

In schools and churches children give pageants and plays that tell the story of the first Christmas.

Scenes, called crèches, show figures of the shepherds and the wise men gathered around the holy family.

Over the years legends have been added to the Christmas story. We suppose that Mary rode a donkey on her way to Bethlehem, though the Bible does not tell us so.

The wise men are sometimes called the three kings. The Bible does not say how many wise men there were. But the legends tell of three, named Caspar, Melchior, and Balthazar. One of them, Balthazar, was dark-skinned, the legends say. People believe that the wise men arrived at the stable in Bethlehem twelve days after Christmas on Twelfth Night. Some say they came on camels; others say on horses.

An ox and an ass, it is said, were in the stable with the holy family. Their breath kept Jesus warm.

Sometimes we hear of other animals.

One is the lamb who gave his wool for Jesus' blanket. Another is the little wren who brought moss and feathers to line the Christ Child's nest.

There is the raven who flew over the stable that first Christmas Eve. He was the first creature to know of Jesus' birth. There is the cock who crowed all that night till dawn.

Many people believe that Jesus was born at midnight. Each Christmas Eve, at this magic hour, animals, they say, kneel to worship and are given the power of human speech. At that hour bees hum the hundredth Psalm.

Animals play such an important part in the Christmas legend that they are treated with special kindness at Christmas. In some countries the cattle and horses are given extra fodder. In Poland they share with the family the bread served at the Christmas feast.

In Scandinavia a sheaf of grain is tied to the top of a tall pole as a feast for the birds. Handsful of grain are strewn for them on walls and rooftops.

In Norway, traps and snares are not set. Fish nets are not placed in the rivers or the sea.

There are different customs in every country. But on Christmas Eve and on Christmas Day, services are held in Christian churches everywhere. Priests and ministers read aloud the Christmas story.

At midnight the bells ring out to announce the hour when Jesus was born. Then people waiting everywhere know that it is Christmas Day.

At Christmastime we decorate our houses with greens. We exchange gifts. We feast and make merry, just as men did long before Jesus was born. But the heart of the Christian winter festival called Christmas is the Christmas story. It is the story of a little boy who was born long ago, in a faraway village, in a stable.

ABOUT THE AUTHOR

Born in Brooklyn, New York, Barbara Cooney grew up on Long Island and in Maine. She received her B.A. degree from Smith College and served as a WAC during World War II. In 1958 Miss Cooney received the Caldecott Medal for *Chanticleer and the Fox*. Miss Cooney lives in a small Massachusetts town with her husband, a physician, and her children.